LAKE DISTRICT

PANORAMAS

Lake District Panoramas

Stunning photographs of England's Lakeland

Photographed by Val Corbett & Robert Grange

Myriad Books

Page 1: River Brathay VC
Previous page: Surprise view,
Derwent Water RG

First published in 2004 by Myriad Books Limited
35 Bishopsthorpe Road, London SE26 4PA

Copyright 2004 © Myriad Books, London

Photographs and text copyright © Val Corbett and Robert Grange

ISBN 1 904154 980

Designed by Cathy Tincknell and Jerry Goldie

Printed in China

Pooley Bridge, Ullswater RG

CONTENTS

NORTH-WEST LAKES

THE NORTH-WEST is "classic" Lakeland containing the Skiddaw hills to the north and the wild crags of Borrowdale to the south. The major town, Keswick, sited on the banks of Derwent Water, is an ideal centre for touring the area. Once away from the town, the region opens up and there are wonderful views, particularly around Derwent Water, Bassenthwaite, Loweswater, Crummock Water and Buttermere.

Map labels:
A595
National Park boundary
A5086
Cockermouth
Bassentwaite Lake
Skiddaw
Keswick
Derwent Water
Loweswater
Crummock Water
Ennerdale
Buttermere
B5289

— Skiddaw reflections —

Tucked away at the north end of Bassenthwaite Lake is a small woodland walk. In among the willows on the foreshore you can catch a glimpse of the lake and valley beyond. The view is always unexpected. I found this mirror-calm image in the afternoon light in January. *RG*

— *Bassenthwaite Lake* —

This dramatic view can usually be glimpsed by travellers on the A66 but few stop, even in the lay-by, to give it a second glance. Here you get an unusual view of the double outlines of Ullock Pike with Skiddaw just showing

over the top. The distinctive shape of Dodd Wood on the right, with the faint detail of the Helvellyn range behind, allow many who know the north Lakes to identify it easily. *RG*

— Derwent Water in winter —

From time to time in recent years, several days of hard frost have left Derwent Water covered with a layer of thick ice. The lake is relatively shallow, especially in the bays, and tends to freeze over faster than other deeper lakes. Launches which leave from Keswick's landing stages normally run throughout the year, but are temporarily put out of service by

the ice, and the usually busy lake is quiet except for the sweeping and scraping of skates and the curious reverberations made by stones being skimmed across the surface. Derwent Island, on the left, is the only inhabited island on the lake and occasionally opens to the public.*VC*

— Catbells from Friar's Crag —

Just a few minutes from Keswick town centre, you wander down to Friar's Crag overlooking the widest lake in the Lake District, Derwentwater. In winter, the old bracken that covers the flanks of Catbells glows orange

at first light, contrasting vividly with the cold blue frost in the rest of the valley. Running left from Catbells you can see Maiden Moor rising into High Spy and then dropping off into Borrowdale. *RG*

— Derwent Water Sunset —

A calm and clear winter's day in the Lake District can be one of the best times of the year. The driving rain and bitter cold is soon forgotten as dramatic views seem to appear on all sides.

Here, a beautiful January day is topped off by a stunning sunset outlining the peaks of Catbells on the left and then Causey Pike, Barrow and Grisedale Pike on the right. *RG*

— *Derwent Water from Castle Head* —

The little hill of Castle Head is one of the nearest low viewpoints in the Lake District. It only takes minutes to climb from Keswick but the views over Derwent Water and the Borrowdale Valley are spectacular. This photograph, taken in late October, shows the view westwards directly across Derwent Water. Prominent fells behind the lake are Maiden

Moor, Catbells, and Causey Pike (with its knobbly profile) on the other side of Newlands Valley. In the foreground of Causey Pike is Barrow, Grasmoor and Grisedale Pike. Launches regularly circumnavigate the lake in both directions, making stops at each of the five jetties. Using the service allows walks of varying lengths to be enjoyed, as an alternative to the long trek around the lake. *VC*

— *Morning mist under Skiddaw* —

Looking north from Ashness landings on Derwent Water the distinctive outline of the Skiddaw range stands high
above Keswick. The deforested Dodd Wood is on the left with the "pimple" shape of Ullock Pike on the Long Side

shoulder, then onto the rounded dome of Carl Side. In the middle is the south end of the ridge that makes up the Skiddaw summit. Then onto Little Man and finally Jenkin Hill as it drops back into the mist. *RG*

— Ashness Bridge —

Taken on a morning in February, the photograph shows ice on the rocks of Barrow Beck which flows under the ancient packhorse bridge on the road to Watendlath. This is one of the Lake District's "treasured views", very popular and photographed by its many visitors. Another such vista, "Surprise View" is just a short distance further up the

same road and gives a fine view over the entire length of Derwent Water. Here the lake is only glimpsed in the far distance, and rising behind it the Skiddaw massif is topped with snow. Most packhorse bridges are extremely narrow and little changed from centuries past. Negotiating them by car takes courage! *VC*

— Watendlath Tarn —

The emphasis in the word "Watendlath" lies on the second syllable "end", contrary to the normal Cumbrian pronunciation where the first syllable is emphasised. Fishing for brown trout is popular on Watendlath Tarn and boats can be hired from the farm in the adjacent hamlet of Watendlath. A packhorse bridge crosses the beck that runs out of

the tarn and ducks and geese busy themselves dabbling in the water. Watendlath is approached along an extremely narrow road. A more pleasurable experience is to walk up, either from Rosthwaite in Borrowdale or by the Lodore waterfalls. The novelist, Hugh Walpole, used Watendlath as the home of his heroine, Judith Paris. *VC*

— Hawes End Sunrise —

Anyone familiar with Beatrix Potter's *Tale of Squirrel Nutkin* might recognise the scene above. In the story, the squirrels would paddle their rafts from Lingholme Woods on the left out to the long dark shape of St Herbert's Island in the

centre to see the Wise Old Owl inside her tree. Now, only ducks paddle in the lake – but red squirrels can still be found throughout the woods of the north Lakes. *RG*

— Derwent Water from Catbells —

This photograph, taken on an early January morning, shows how colourful the Lake District can be even in the middle of winter. Originally this landscape would have looked very different. Once, the fells up to 2,000 feet or so would have been tree-covered but early clearances led to impoverishment of the soil and eventually bracken grew in place of the trees. Although

unproductive, the bracken turns a glorious colour in the autumn, which lasts until new growth starts again in the spring. Catbells is in the foreground of the photo and the view includes Bassenthwaite Lake in the far distance on the left. The Skiddaw massif, with Blencathra to the right, forms a backdrop to Keswick and the northern reaches of Derwent Water. *VC*

— Buttermere —

For many years these Scots pines have stood at the top of Buttermere overlooking Gatesgarth Beck. Towering above the flat land at the top of the lake is High Crag, Haystacks and Fleetwith Pike, all surrounding Warnscale Bottom.

Look closely and you can just see the cloud creeping over the crags in the middle of the picture, showing how different the weather can be between valley floor and mountain top. *RG*

— Melbreak from Crummock Water —

From the tranquil south shore of Crummock Water you can see the sugar- dusted profile of Melbreak. This is one of the Lake District's quieter mountains. Unlike most Cumbrian fells it stands alone. It is a lengthy walk in and its steep, formidable sides attract only the most dedicated and hardened walkers. *RG*

— *Grasmoor and Rannerdale* —

A late afternoon in September gave me the chance to capture this spectacular view. It stretches from the boathouse in Lanthwaite woods surrounded by amazing autumn colours to the imposing Grasmoor with its weatherbeaten west face

then on down to Rannerdale and Rannerdale Knotts, where the road lurches round the corner into Buttermere. Crossing the valley in the mist, you can see High Stile and Red Pike, and finally shafts of sunlight poking over the shoulder of Melbreak. *RG*

— *Loweswater Valley and Crummock Water* —

The view to the east from the relatively modest summit of Low Fell is particularly extensive.
To the left, the steep sides of Grasmoor are echoed on the right by the slopes of Melbreak. The lake between the two
is Crummock Water. Buttermere, out of sight, lies in a cradle of mountains beyond. The distinctive profile of Great Gable

is seen in the far distance. Loweswater Church and the Kirkstile Inn, although lower on the valley floor, still enjoy
magnificent views. Loweswater Show, one of the best of the traditional shepherds' events, is held
in a nearby field in September. *VC*

— Loweswater reflections —

Loweswater hides at the most north-westerly edge of the Lake District. It is a small lake which empties into Crummock Water under the gaze of Burnbank and Darling Fell. Tucked into the southern side is Holme Wood, famous for its bluebells in spring and its autumn colours. Here it is catching the sun on a winter's morning. *RG*

— Loweswater —

Rowing boats for fishing belong to the National Trust and can be hired at Watergate Farm at the southern tip of Loweswater. Anglers can fish for trout, perch and pike. Also from this point a walk leads through the attractive woodland on the lake's west shore. The name "Loweswater" means "the leafy lake" and this name probably derives

from the nearby wood. In the photograph the prominent fell to the left is called Low Fell. Despite this name it enjoys spectacular views which can be seen in the Loweswater Valley and Crummock Water photograph on page 36. Grasmoor is in the far distance on the right. *VC*

NORTH-EAST LAKES

WITH ULLSWATER AND HAWESWATER at its heart, the
north-east corner of the Lake District contains a wealth of
glorious locations and classic Lakeland scenery. Ullswater, with
its wooded slopes and winding banks is almost pastoral when
compared with the dramatic reservoir of Haweswater framed by
its white stones surrounded by bare fells. At the dale end of
Haweswater is the dramatic range of High Street – fells traversed
by an old Roman road.

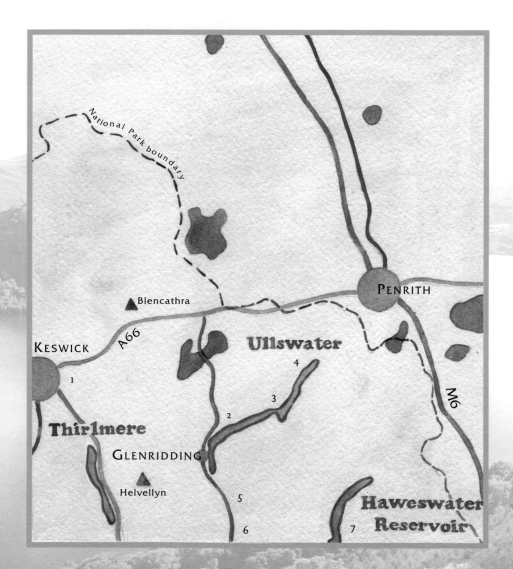

— Castlerigg stone circle —

As one of the most complete stone circles in the country, Castlerigg always attracts attention. Many speculate that it was an important market for axe heads mined just south of here. Others say that it was a site for religious ceremonies.

Whatever its purpose, Castlerigg is a bitterly cold place to visit in winter. It consists of 38 standing stones, some of them 8ft (2.4m) high, forming a circle 100ft (30m) in diameter. *RG*

— *Ullswater dawn* —

Anglers and photographers are generally the only people to be found on the shoreline of Ullswater enjoying
the dawn. Early mist, which gathers across the lake, is gently dissolved as the sun rises. This view from
Glencoyne looks east towards the slopes of Place Fell with Hallin Fell beyond. Any long walk along this

eastern road-free stretch of the lake is best done with the help of one of Ullswater's steamers. A good route is to catch a boat to the jetty at Howtown and walk through Auterstone wood to Pooley Bridge, where there is another steamer pier. *VC*

— *Ullswater* —

Sitting on the bench above Yew Crags gives you a view of the entire length of Ullswater. Starting at Pooley Bridge on the left you can follow the Roman road called High Street. It traverses the ridgeline over Barton Fell to Loadpot Hill above

Martindale. Then it disappears behind High Dodd and Place Fell on the eastern shores of the lake. At the top of the lake, just in view, is Silver Point and Glenridding. Above is Stony Cove and then beyond that the southern end of the Helvellyn range. *RG*

— Ullswater boathouse —

Ullswater is the Lake District's second largest lake. Thanks to a speed limit of 10mph for boat traffic, the lake remains relatively peaceful. In summer Ullswater is pretty with the colourful sails of windsurfers, dinghies and yachts. At either end of the lake it is possible to hire rowing boats and little motorboats.

This view from the flatter landscape at the northern end near to Pooley Bridge looks across to Arthur's Pike and Bonscale Pike, both good destinations for a quiet fell walk. The name of Ullswater derives from Ulfr, a Norse settler who was the first Lord of Ullswater. *VC*

— *Angle Tarn* —

Not to be confused with the Angle Tarn under Bowfell, this Angle Tarn lies high above Patterdale and Hartsop.
The Tarn has a gentler appearance than many of the high tarns, being attractively cupped by surrounding crags
and unusually indented and reedy. Fine views to the west can be gained by a short climb and seen in this photo in

the far distance are the more northerly stretches of the Helvellyn range. The route of Wainwright's Coast to Coast walk passes the tarn, which in itself makes a justifiably popular destination for walks from the Patterdale valley. *VC*

— High Street —

A wall runs along a considerable length of High Street, the course of a Roman road which linked the forts
at Brougham near Penrith to Galava at Ambleside, a distance of 28 miles. Nowadays the bridleway is
popular with walkers and cyclists. Roman roads commonly ran along the unforested summits of the fells,

giving easier marching and better protection from brigands. The mountain of High Street, seen on the right in the distance, has a flat summit and used to be the site for horse races giving rise to its alternative name of Racecourse Hill. *VC*

— *Haweswater* —

Reflections of the fells in the water on a calm winter's morning give Haweswater a peaceful air.
However, submerged beneath the water lies the old village of Mardale, which was drowned after the
Haweswater dam was completed in the late 1930s to supply Manchester with water. The valley's church, pub,

houses and farms were all flooded. In recent years, drought conditions have allowed the water level to fall sufficiently for the remains of the village to be seen. The mountains in view are, from the left, Mardale Ill Bell, High Street (with the Long Stile ridge and The Rigg in the foreground) and Kidsty Pike. *VC*

SOUTH-WEST LAKES

THE SOUTH-WEST is the most thinly populated part of the Lake District. As you travel west, there are very few towns or major roads and the scenery becomes more rugged. This wild landscape contains England's deepest lake, Wast Water at 200ft (61m) and its highest mountain – Scafell Pike which rises to 3,209 feet (978m). The views across Wast Water to the three peaks of Scafell, Scafell Pike and Bowfell are dramatic.

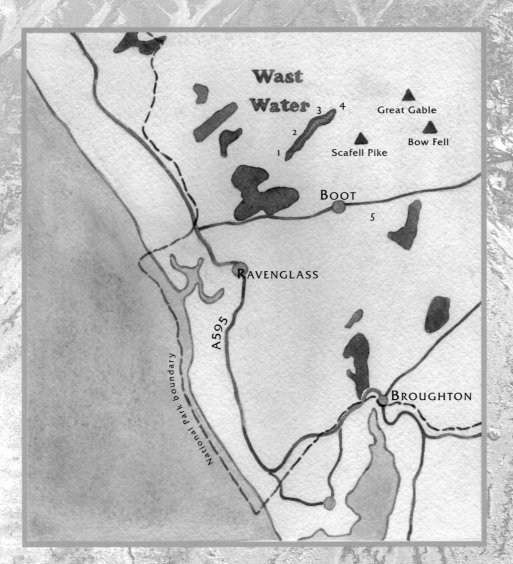

— *Wastwater* —

Quintessential Lakeland, the central section of this classic view of Wastwater is used as the logo for the Lake District National Park Authority. The grandeur of the surrounding fells is hard to better, and it is arguably the most dramatic view in the Lake District. From left to right the fells in view are Yewbarrow, Kirk Fell, Great Gable,

Scafell and the Wasdale Screes. Wastwater is the deepest lake, and Scafell Pike (just out of view) the highest mountain in England. The lake is open to the west, and for most of the year enjoys particularly good evening light. *VC*

— *Wasdale Screes* —

The Screes form a dramatic mile-long wall on the south side of Wastwater which contrasts sharply with the gentler shoreline opposite. The overall drop amounts to nearly 2,000ft (610m). Although the Screes look sheer, an awkward footpath follows the lakeshore while an airy path traverses the top. The entire length of the Screes is riven by steep

gullies, which offer challenging routes for the mountaineer. Greathall Ghyll at the western end forms an interesting geological boundary and is accessible on foot. The steep and crumbling gullies offer a habitat for rare and interesting plants such as the shrubby cinquefoil. *VC*

— Scafell Pike —

Seen from the shores of Wastwater, three mountains stand out in simple grandeur. On the left is Lingmell, smooth and rounded, dropping back on to the crags that make up this side of Scafell Pike at 3,205ft (977m). Tucked away in the shadow is Mickledore and Broad Stand (the coll between Scafell Pike and Scafell). Finally, you come to the smoother lines of Scafell topping out at 3,163ft (964m). Straight ahead are the darker folds of Rakehead Crag and the brown scorched grass of early spring. *RG*

— *Wasdale Head* —

The track at Wasdale Head leads to some of the Lake District's greatest fells. The western face of Great Gable, seen ahead, has classic climbing routes. On the left of the track, surrounded by ancient yews, is the tiny church of St Olaf's.
In the graveyard there are memorials to climbers and inside a beautiful stained-glass window showing the dramatic rock

formation of nearby Napes Needle with the dedication "I will lift up mine eyes unto the hills from whence cometh my strength". The Wasdale Show, held at the beginning of October, takes place in adjacent fields. Highlights are the races up Kirk Fell, shown on the left of the photograph. *VC*

— *Brotherilkeld Farm, Eskdale* —

This photograph of Brotherilkeld Farm and the Upper Eskdale valley was taken from the slopes of Harter Fell on a late October afternoon. Some of the giants of the Lake District mountains are in view at the end of the valley – Scafell, Scafell Pike, Esk Pike, Bowfell and Crinkle Crags. On the far right of the photograph, just above the road

up to Hardknott Pass, is the dramatically sited Roman fort of Hardknott, probably founded under Hadrian. This guarded the strategic Roman road which ran from the then major supply harbour at Ravenglass on the coast, over the mountains to Ambleside. *VC*

SOUTH-EAST LAKES

THE SOUTH-EAST quarter of the Lake District enjoys enchanting scenery around Coniston Water and, at its western edge, in the Langdales. Coniston has strong literary connections: the romantic poet, William Wordsworth, went to grammar school in Hawkshead and, his most famous home, Dove Cottage, is in Grasmere. John Ruskin, the author, art critic and social reformer lived at Brantwood on the shores of Coniston. Coniston is the setting for much of Arthur Ransome's much-loved children's novel, *Swallows and Amazons*. And, of course, Beatrix Potter made her home at Hill Top. The south-east also contains the popular towns of Ambleside, Windermere and Bowness. Lake Windermere itself, despite its popularity, remains a beautiful and charming stretch of water with many hidden treasures away from the hustle and bustle of the main towns.

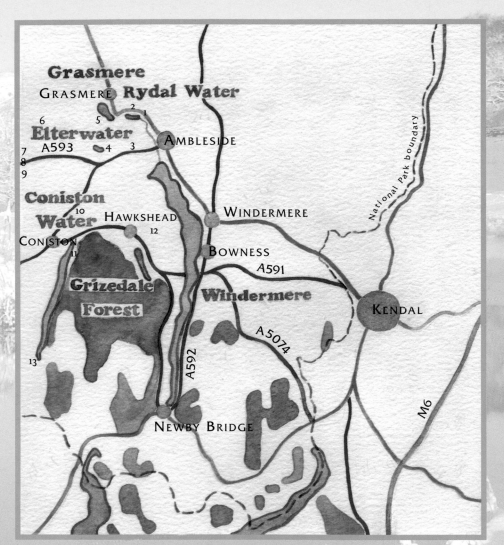

Grasmere

GRASMERE **Rydal Water**

Grasmere

6

5

2 1

Elterwater

A593 4 3

7

8

9

AMBLESIDE

Coniston Water

10

HAWKSHEAD

12

CONISTON

11

WINDERMERE

BOWNESS

A591

Grizedale Forest

Windermere

A592

A5074

KENDAL

13

NEWBY BRIDGE

M6

National Park boundary

— *Rydal Water Dawn* —

As you travel from Ambleside north on the main road on a late summer morning, you will catch this view of Rydal Water. The lake is often shrouded in mist and, when it is, it has an almost magical feel. Heron Island, the largest in the lake, is silhouetted against the morning sun. I can think of no better place to be. *RG*

— Rydal Water misty —

Looking west along Rydal Water you can see the many little islands that go to make this one of the most
picturesque areas in the Lake District. In autumn the valleys here are often shrouded in mist until late in the

morning. But when the mist lifts, it does so very quickly – 10 minutes before this photograph was taken, it was impossible to see clearly for more than 20 feet in any direction. *RG*

— *Windermere dawn* —

September is the best month for enjoying the drifting beauty of mist lying over the lakes. The view south over Windermere, taken from the lower slopes of Loughrigg Fell, is particularly lovely at dawn. Waterhead, on the lakeside at Ambleside lies hidden quietly beneath the mist but later in the day is busy with passengers embarking

on lake cruises or hiring boats. At this time of the year a swimming race takes place from Wray Castle on the west of the lake back to Waterhead. Windermere is the longest of the lakes, over 10 miles long, and the largest lake in England. *VC*

— River Brathay —

The lazy broad waters of the River Brathay as it leaves Elterwater contrast sharply with the rushing beck that flows from Little Langdale, over Colwith Force and into Elterwater. The Norse word Brathay means "broad river". Elterwater means "swan lake" and swans are commonly seen around the mouth of the river. The

Brathay flows eventually into Windermere, a mile or so to the east, at the point where Galava, the Roman Fort, is situated. The Cumbria Way, traversing the entire county from south to north, passes along this stretch of river bank. *VC*

— *Loughrigg Tarn* —

Nestled at the foot of the Langdale Valley, up above Skelwith Bridge, is Loughrigg Tarn. This beautiful pocket of the
lakes is a haven of peace and tranquillity. Let your gaze wander over the water lilies and the white geese to the
Langdale Pikes beyond. *RG*

— Lower Langdale —

This area has been important for centuries. Above, on the right, you will find the ancient quarries which provided a ready supply of high quality stone for axe heads many thousands of years ago. These were sold far and wide and

have been found all over the British Isles in different archaeological sites. Down and to the left (just out of the picture) is a large rock with ancient rock carvings. Less than a minute from the road, it is a site worth visiting. *RG*

— *Upper Langdale* —

Looking north from below Blea Tarn into the heart of the Lakeland fells, you can see the u-shaped valleys left by the glaciers. The deep blue sky on a hot spring day outlines the high peaks. On the right appears Harrison Stickle, the Langdale Pikes and then Pike of Stickle. The ridge then drops down to Black Crag and Rossett

Crag. You can then see Bowfell hiding behind the Buttress of "The Band", in the middle of the valley. Still going left along the ridge, you will find Shelter Crag and Crinkle Crags. Then, above the dark mass of Kettle Crag on the left is Pike of Blisco. *RG*

— *Little Langdale* —

Early morning November sun lights up the dead bracken on the slopes around Little Langdale Tarn. This valley, owned by the National Trust, successfully retains its traditional character and only light traffic uses the narrow

road to Wrynose Pass. The tarn itself is inaccessible but a popular footpath passes over the picturesque little stone Slaters Bridge, which crosses the infant River Brathay soon after it leaves the tarn. *VC*

— Blea Tarn —

Blea Tarn lies on higher ground between the two valleys of Great Langdale and Little Langdale, and is surrounded by colourful rhododendrons in the summer. On the day this photograph was taken, little "islands" of snow had been sent scudding across the lake by the wind to make single lines on the near

shore. The Tarn is exceptionally accessible, with an adjacent car park and a wheelchair friendly track. The Langdale Pikes are in the far distance with the distinctive peaks of Pike of Stickle on the left and Harrison Stickle on the right. *VC*

— Tarn Hows —

Winter does little to dampen the appeal of this ever-popular beauty spot. Well-managed car parks and footpaths under the care of the National Trust ensure that the tarn is protected from being spoilt by the pressure of visitor numbers. Tarn Hows itself was once a series of smaller tarns but a little dam was built and the land flooded,

creating just the single tarn. In an elevated position well above Hawkshead and Coniston, the land around the tarn has extensive panoramas. In this view the Langdale Pikes can be seen on the left, and the fells comprising the Fairfield horseshoe on the right. *VC*

— Coniston —

This view, looking westward across the lake of Coniston, is similar to the one John Ruskin, writer, critic and social reformer, would have enjoyed from his house Brantwood just a little way further down the lake. He described it as having "on the whole, the finest view of Cumberland or Lancashire." A ferry service connects Brantwood with

Coniston and the National Trust's restored steam yacht *The Gondola* runs a service around the lake in the summer.
The bulk of The Old Man of Coniston mountain dominates the slate grey village of Coniston. High Bank Ground,
the farm in the foreground, was the setting for Arthur Ransome's *Swallows and Amazons*. VC

— View from Latterbarrow —

A short sharp climb from a lane near Hawskhead leads to the summit of Latterbarrow, one of the best of the lower panoramic viewpoints in the southern Lake District. The vista to the west, across Hawkshead to the Coniston Fells, is impressive but this is the spectacular view taking in Blelham Tarn and its sylvan surroundings

with the northern reaches of Lake Windermere. Ambleside lies at the furthest end of Windermere, and the bulky fell behind is Red Screes. Wansfell, in shadow, is to the far right and the Fairfield Horseshoe is clearly identifiable in the middle left. *VC*

— *Kelly Hall Tarn* —

This quiet tarn lies only a short distance from the road running up the west side of Coniston Water. Close to the village of Torver, the area is known as Torver Back Common, land that is owned by the Lake District National Park Authority. Some of the Coniston Fells are shown in the photo, including Dow Crag and The Old Man of Coniston towards the right. A good approach for walkers to the Fells is from Torver, starting on the Walna Scar Road, a bridleway. A branch to the right eventually passes Goats Water with its impressive backdrop of climbing crags. *VC*